DC

D0590641

2

DOWSING

SHIRLEY WALLIS

ELEMENT

Shaftesbury, Dorset • Boston, Massachusetts • Melbourne, Victoria

© Element Books Limited 1999

First published in Great Britain in 1999 by
ELEMENT BOOKS LIMITED
Shaftesbury, Dorset SP7 8BP

Published in the USA in 1999 by
ELEMENT BOOKS INC.
160 North Washington Street, Boston, MA 02114

Published in Australia in 1999 by
ELEMENT BOOKS
and distributed by Penguin Australia Ltd.
487 Maroondah Highway, Ringwood, Victoria 3134

Designed and created for Element Books with
The Bridgewater Book Company

ELEMENT BOOKS LIMITED
Managing Editor *Miranda Spicer*
Senior Commissioning Editor *Caro Ness*
Project Editor *Kate John*
Group Production Director *Clare Armstrong*
Production Manager *Susan Sutterby*
Production Controller *Linsey Denholm*

THE BRIDGEWATER BOOK COMPANY
Art Director *Terry Jeavons*
Designer *Alison Honey*
Editorial Director *Sophie Collins*
Managing Editor *Anne Townley*
Project Editor *Caroline Earle*
Picture Research *Lynda Marshall*
Studio Photography *Mike Hemsley, Walter Gardiner Photography*
Illustrations *Rhian Nest James*
Endpapers *Sarah Young*

Printed and bound in the UK by Butler & Tanner, Frome

British Library Cataloguing in Publication
data available

Library of Congress Cataloging in Publication data available

ISBN: 1-86204-486-4

Picture credits:
AKG, London: front cover, 7t; British Society of Dowsers: front cover, 4;
Fortean Picture Library: 5, 54–55; Image Bank: 48; Stock Market: 7b, 38b, 39, 46.

Models: Gavin Bates, Clare Bayes

CONTENTS

WHAT IS DOWSING?

Dowsing is the skill of seeking answers and interpreting them using metal or wooden rods, or a pendulum. Today, dowsing is widely used as a simple but effective tool of search-and-discovery for anything from lost coins to geophysical surveys.

DOWSING FOR BOOBY TRAPS

Skilled dowsers are employed by police forces, large oil and mining organizations, and also farmers and water companies, forced by increasing worldwide drought to seek alternative underground sources of water. During the war in Vietnam, American engineers used dowsing rods to detect booby traps and tunnels, and other military organizations are known to have employed dowsing for surveying.

The art of dowsing can be successfully learned by anyone who is willing to focus, experiment, and practice their responses. A few people can manage without rods, using just their hands and being sensitive to their body's reactions to a given target.

You don't need to be psychic to learn how to dowse. As long as you have common sense and an inquiring mind you are well on the way to acquiring a useful, varied, and practical skill.

MOST DOWSERS EMPLOY RODS, ALTHOUGH IT IS POSSIBLE TO USE JUST THE HANDS.

SUCCESSFUL DOWSING HAS A LONG HISTORY

Dowsing (or divining) has been used for many centuries and by many different civilizations, mostly by people searching for water and minerals.

In the fifth century B.C.E. the Scythians of southern Russia were described as using willow rods for divining by Herodotus, a Greek writer. There are dowsing references in Chinese literature from as long ago as 2200 B.C.E., and rock paintings in the Central Sahara from around 3000 B.C.E. depict what also seems to be dowsing. It occurs, too, on Egyptian bas-reliefs, which emphasizes the fact that the most important commodity in this arid region, then as now, is water.

The German scholar Georgius Agricola (1494–1555), known as the father of mineralogy, gives details of procedures for dowsing and detecting new mineral lodes in his valuable work *De Re Metallica*. Queen Elizabeth I of England (1533–1603) implemented a policy to encourage German miners to take their dowsing expertise to the mining communities in England, but it was only during the reign of James I (1603–25), that this project finally bore fruit.

DIVINING FOR METAL, A SIXTEENTH-CENTURY ENGRAVING FROM *DE RE METALLICA* BY GEORGIUS AGRICOLA.

In 1693, Pierre Le Lorraine, the Abbé de Vallemont, recognizing that the ability to dowse differed from one person to the next, realized that the key factor in explaining how dowsing worked was the connection between the dowser and the target.

THE MINERALOGIST GEORGIUS AGRICOLA OUTLINED THE USE OF DOWSING FOR MINERALS IN HIS BOOK *DE RE METALLICA*.

He wrote a treatise on the subject, which was suppressed by the Holy See in 1702.

In 1692, Jacques Aymer, a dowser of some repute, was hired to track down the murderers of a wine merchant and his wife from Lyons. His work culminated in the capture of one of the culprits and resulted in a considerable amount of interest in dowsing in France during the following century.

Around the same time Jesuit priests were also investigating the techniques and recording their findings. Among them, Fathers Athanasius Kirscher and Bernard Caesius wrote papers concluding that the involuntary muscle action of a dowser was responsible for a result.

PENDULUMS ARE JUST AS EFFECTIVE AS RODS, AND ARE POPULAR TODAY.

HOW DOES IT WORK?

The mysteries of dowsing are activated by the interaction between divining rods or a pendulum, and the human body. Dowsing is a bridge between your body and the outside world.

ENERGY FIELDS

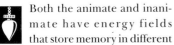

Both the animate and inanimate have energy fields that store memory in different ways. Everything that exists in the universe is ultimately pure energy. This is a central belief of Taoist and Buddhist philosophies that has been demonstrated in our own time by those working in the field of quantum mechanics who have taken matter and measured and reduced it to vibrational frequency. This includes every particle, thought, word, emotion, object, and experience. When you dowse for a target you are really tuning into its frequency. The response from the rods or pendulum shows clearly that you are reflecting energy back to yourself for interpretation.

THE HUMAN BODY

We all possess an energy field that radiates life force and absorbs radiations from the environment. It is a unique package of anatomy and physiology surrounded by an electromagnetic field called the aura. Invisible to normal sight, emanations from the aura can be seen with Kirlian photography or on a video screen attached to an electrocrystal scanner held over the body. The aura usually extends about 3.2 ft. (1m) around the physical body in a colorful movement. It shows the vibrations of the inner energy centers (chakras), their pathways (meridians), and the subtle bodies, so-called because they are composed of finer substance than physical matter.

BRAIN POWER

Scientists who have studied the two hemispheres of the human brain say that the left side codes memory in verbal and analytical thought and the right side specializes in understanding opaque patterns and responding to intuition.

Tuning in to your intuitional nature helps develop greater dowsing sensitivity in your body, which connects with the psychic vibrations from dowsing rods or a pendulum. The instruments simply become a physical extension of yourself, and so you develop a response-ability for your actions.

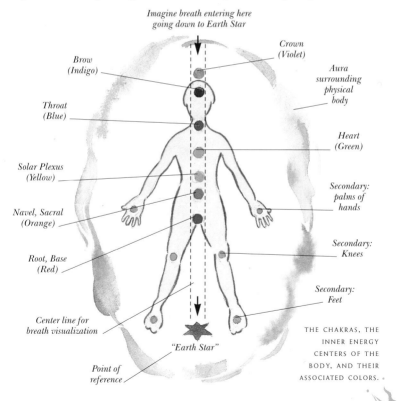

Imagine breath entering here going down to Earth Star

Crown (Violet)

Brow (Indigo)

Aura surrounding physical body

Throat (Blue)

Heart (Green)

Solar Plexus (Yellow)

Secondary: palms of hands

Navel, Sacral (Orange)

Secondary: Knees

Root, Base (Red)

Secondary: Feet

Center line for breath visualization

"Earth Star"

Point of reference

THE CHAKRAS, THE INNER ENERGY CENTERS OF THE BODY, AND THEIR ASSOCIATED COLORS.

ESTABLISHING A CODE OF PRACTICE

 Dowsing can be experienced at many levels, from games on a rainy day to serious scientific research, but whatever the activity, the response-ability is yours and success comes only from good preparation. When dowsing, always follow this code of practice.

1 RELAXATION

Before you start, a relaxed attitude in mind and body is very important. Dowsing should not be attempted when tired, ill, or stressed since your results could be impaired. Dowsing uses up a lot of energy, so avoid long sessions. Have clear positive motives, wear comfortable clothes, discard your watch, rings, jewelry, metallic objects including any keys and coins in your pockets, and do not carry a knapsack or bag when dowsing anywhere. The aim is relaxed concentration. Avoid interruptions such as the doorbell or telephone, and discourage onlookers.

2 AURA PROTECTION/ ALIGNMENT

Aura protection may seem unusual but it's important, particularly when working outdoors, because there are many invisible energies through which you may pass that can affect you. These can sometimes distort your aura or drain your energy, making you tired and irritable. Take a deep breath and imagine it entering through the crown of your head. As you exhale, visualize a line drawing down through the center of your body to a depth of about 6in. (15cm) below your feet. With a second breath down from the crown, imagine clear white-violet light filling your aura, above, below, in front of you, behind, to the left and right, and all around you. You have now centered and protected yourself, while remaining relaxed.

3 CHECK PENDULUM YES/NO RESPONSES

Check your pendulum responses before every dowsing session since these sometimes change (see The Pendulum, pages 16–20).

4 PERMISSION TO PROCEED

Before you begin, make sure the circumstances and your ethical approach are correct for the task by asking yourself the following question through the pendulum: Am I ready to proceed?

A negative response now can save time. Try again later if this happens.

Remember to obtain permission:
a) from landowners if you propose dowsing on private land,
b) from people who may feel imposed upon or interfered with if your activities seem to invade their living space or body energies.

5 EXPERIMENT AND PRACTICE
Start your inquiry with simple targets, which, in turn, demand simple questions.

6 RECORD YOUR ACTIVITIES
It is very useful for future reference to keep a journal to record your sessions, activities, and progress.

1 START BY REMOVING ALL METAL OBJECTS FROM YOUR PERSON.

2 CENTER YOURSELF BY VISUALIZING CLEAR LIGHT ENTERING YOUR AURA FROM ABOVE.

3 KEEP A RECORD OF YOUR SESSIONS AND HOW THEY HAVE PROGRESSED.

THE TOOLS OF THE DOWSER

Some people are happy to use a pendulum for dowsing, others opt for rods;
experienced dowsers usually prefer to use a combination of both. Beginners
need to ascertain what works best for them by experiment and practice.

PENDULUM

As a guide, keep in mind a builder's plumb bob hanging from a plumb line to find a vertical position: it is a symmetrical-shaped weight with a pointed base, well-balanced, and able to swing freely from a cord or chain. Any materials are suitable – wood, crystal, or metal. Size and weight are determined by the use to which you put it: small for close, specific work such as map-reading or diagnosing health problems; heavier with a longer cord for outdoor work. Avoid using personal jewelry that is in constant use because it absorbs your energy, which may alter its sensitivity. Likewise, don't wear your pendulum, but keep it separate in a little container.

RODS

The two basic types are the traditional Y-shaped rod or a forked stick cut from a resilient wood such as hazel or willow (or made from metal) and L-shaped rods or angle rods of wire or metal held one in each hand. A single rod called a bobber, held by its lighter end, is very effective for some people and can be made or purchased. Rods are more often used outdoors for detecting underground targets and for onsite or earth-energy investigations. Heavier metal/steel rods are more robust in breezy weather.

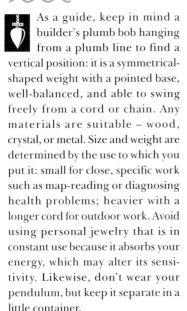

MOST MATERIALS
ARE SUITABLE FOR
A PENDULUM.

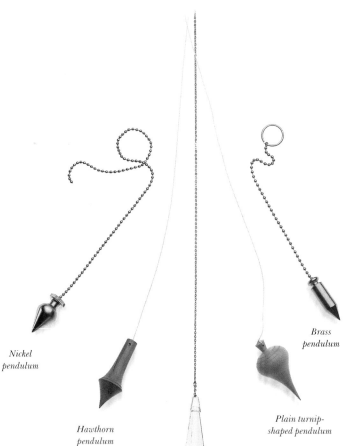

Nickel pendulum

Hawthorn pendulum

Crystal pendulum

Brass pendulum

Plain turnip-shaped pendulum

THE PENDULUM

Always select the pendulum yourself because it is a personal extension of your being and you must allow yourself to be guided instinctively to the material that suits your nature. Purchase one or make your own.

WOOD

 Can be bought ready made or a wood turner can make you a well-balanced shape; make sure a small size is not too light. A larger type, such as the old-fashioned wooden spinning top, is used in advanced techniques and is called the long pendulum. It usually has a long holding string of natural fiber and by holding it at different lengths can be used to seek hidden substances. Water responds to a 26-in. (65-cm) string. Wooden pendulums sometimes have a hollow center to take search samples. If you're looking for plastic piping, for instance, place a sample in the pendulum: like attracts like.

CRYSTAL

 For general purposes, a single-terminated, clear quartz crystal capped with a ring to hold a chain or cord is ideal. Quartz receives and transmits energy. All semiprecious stones and gems have different qualities and vibrations that are worth looking into, especially if you feel drawn to healing or health dowsing. Lead crystal or chandelier pendants, displaying rainbows in sunlight, can enhance your environment.

CHOOSE A
PENDULUM MATERIAL
THAT SUITS YOU.

METAL

Brass, copper, and chrome pendulums can be purchased and are excellent for map dowsing or close diagnostic work. In an emergency, be inventive and think "pendulum." A thread holding a button or a needle, a small plastic ball on a string – knot one end of the string, puncture the ball and insert the string – a key on a chain: just about anything can work for a positively-minded dowser.

IF IN THE RIGHT
FRAME OF MIND
YOU CAN DOWSE
WITH A BUTTON ON
A THREAD.

A HOUSE KEY TIED
TO A CHAIN HAS
OFTEN BEEN
PRESSED INTO USE
IN AN EMERGENCY.

GETTING STARTED
AND TUNING IN

 To connect with your body's positive and negative energy-fields, hold the pendulum string or chain between the forefinger and thumb of the writing hand. Allow approximately 4–6in. (10–15cm) between pendulum and fingertip, whatever feels comfortable. Start it moving gently by letting the pendulum swing forward and backward over the right thigh if you're right-handed, left thigh if left-handed.

Now ask the question:

Show me my swing for YES.

The pendulum will settle and make a change, very often to a clockwise motion. Whatever the direction, this is your YES signal.

Now repeat the process over the other thigh asking the question:

Show me my swing for NO.

Note the direction. This time it may be a counterclockwise motion or swing at a consistent angle. Nothing happened? Take a deep breath, center your energies and try again. If still nothing happens, program your brain thus: sit at a table, draw a circle of about 3in. (6–7cm) in diameter and mark it as shown in the diagram opposite. Let your pendulum swing back and forth over the NEUTRAL position. Program this into your mind by repeating to yourself:

*This is the neutral
and scanning position.*

Now set the pendulum in a clockwise direction and repeat several times to yourself:

This is for YES.

Turn the pendulum into a counter-clockwise direction and repeat several times:

This is for NO.

Looking at the diagram again, practice and absorb the swing directions marked for the *YES/But* and the

THE CHAIN/STRING IS
HELD BETWEEN THE
THUMB AND FOREFINGER
POINTING DOWNWARD.

NO/But answers. This answer from your pendulum is very useful because it indicates that the question you are asking needs to be more specific. It is saying: *Yes... we are on the right lines but rephrase please.*

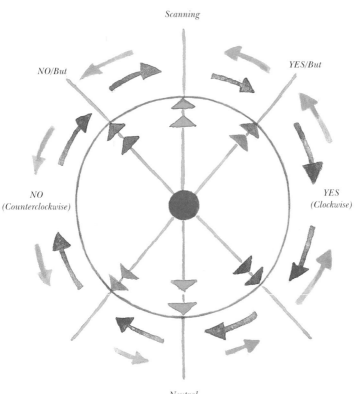

Scanning

NO/But

YES/But

NO
(Counterclockwise)

YES
(Clockwise)

Neutral
Position

TO PROGRAM YOURSELF, HOLD THE PENDULUM OVER THE CENTER
AND SWING IT BACK AND FORTH ALONG THE SCANNING LINE. NOW
CLOCKWISE FOR YES. THEN COUNTERCLOCKWISE FOR NO. FINALLY
ACROSS THE ANGLE FOR YES/BUT... AND NO/BUT...

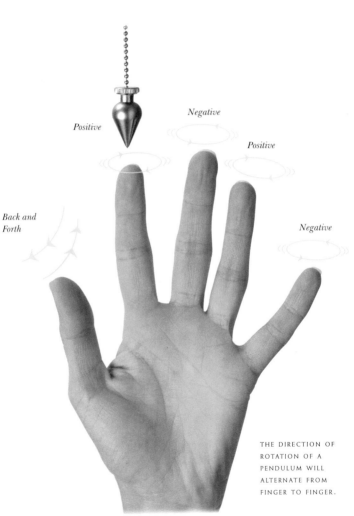

Positive

Negative

Positive

Back and Forth

Negative

THE DIRECTION OF
ROTATION OF A
PENDULUM WILL
ALTERNATE FROM
FINGER TO FINGER.

THE FINGER TEST

Try this exercise in allowing the pendulum to speak to you – about you. Breathe in and center yourself. With your pendulum ready, raise your free hand with the fingers pointing upward, supporting your elbow on a table or against your body. Hold the pendulum approximately 1in. (2.54cm) above the forefinger and let it swing freely. Once you get a reaction, repeat the exercise over the second, third, and little fingers, noting each direction of the pendulum's flow. Finally, the thumb. The fingers should alternate positive/negative (YES/NO) except the thumb, which usually reacts in a neutral or different way – perhaps swinging back and forth.

Now perform the test on a member of the opposite sex and see if there is a difference. Some people's fingers will respond in a similar way, while others may show variations.

If you had any doubts about the energy we radiate, then this reveals the streams coming through our hands to our fingers. Likewise, the energy of the aura, chakras, and meridians can be detected by a trained practitioner.

It is unwise to experiment with your pendulum over the human body – especially the chakra areas – since such activity can interfere with a person's energy field if you are untrained. The six chakra areas to avoid are the crown of the head, the third eye position between the eyes on the forehead, the throat, the heart position on the center of the chest, the navel, and the genitals. However, do practice around the auras of indoor and outdoor plants: they respond in different ways to their location through the geomagnetic force of the earth, so you can test which table or sill suits the plant best – it will tell you.

EVEN A PLANT HAS AN AURA. YOU CAN EXPERIMENT TO FIND THE POSITION THAT SUITS IT BEST.

ASKING THE RIGHT QUESTIONS

The key to success is: always bear in mind the letters SS. They stand for Simple and Specific. Train yourself to think in terms of questions that invite Yes/No answers, pose them carefully, and make them direct. For example, you have mislaid your keys.

You can't say: *Where are my keys?*
Instead say:
Are my keys in the house? YES
Are they in the kitchen? NO
Living room? NO
My bedroom? YES
In the closet? YES
In a pocket? NO
In a purse? YES/But
In a bag? YES

WRITING DOWN YOUR QUESTIONS CAN HELP YOU TO LEARN TO PHRASE THEM SIMPLY AND SPECIFICALLY.

You rush to the closet and remember dropping them in the bag with your new shoes when you got home laden with shopping. The pendulum focused the memory for you.

Another approach to this problem would be: first establish the house as your focus. Then go to each room in turn asking:

Are the keys here?

A lengthier process. Work from the point of inquiry as much as you can. Writing down questions may help you get into SS mode.

REMEMBER THAT A PENDULUM WILL ONLY GIVE YES AND NO OR YES/BUT AND NO/BUT ANSWERS.

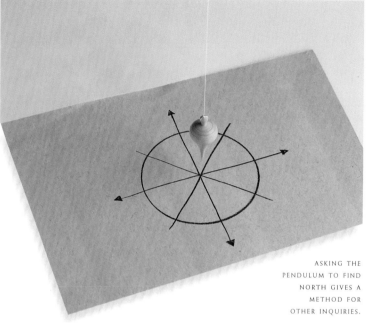

ASKING THE
PENDULUM TO FIND
NORTH GIVES A
METHOD FOR
OTHER INQUIRIES.

SCANNING

 Find a sample of your target and "show" it to the pendulum using the scanning movement that you have already established for yourself (*see page 16*).

Say: *This is a sample of the target.*

Let the pendulum swing over it for a moment. Now ask something like:

Is this material/substance in the room?

DIRECTION

 Draw a circle and divide it into the directions of the compass. Let the pendulum scan it first and get to "feel" it. Then ask a question such as:

Where is magnetic north from here?

Watch the line of the swing for your answer. Use this method to ascertain the direction for any inquiry with the pendulum.

DOWSING RODS

Rods are generally used outdoors for tracing water, minerals, and earth energies in the landscape particularly at sacred sites, and for geopathic lines connected with buildings.

HOW TO MAKE YOUR RODS

They can be made of wood, like the traditional forked twig or Y-rod, but you can also use various metals, spring steel, or even plastic that won't snap under great stress. Water diviners sometimes find the tension on their forked wooden rod leads to breakage, but still prefer to use the natural material. Likewise, the single rod, or bobber, is available ready-made or you can make one yourself from tensile materials that include wood.

Choosing the correct type of rods to suit your needs comes with experience, but to begin with, the simplest are the L-shaped variety, sometimes called angle irons, which are a matching pair of rods held parallel to each other by the shorter length.

Angle irons can be bought from a store, iron ones can be specially forged, or you can make them yourself from any kind of wire such as fencing wire or wire coathangers.

L-SHAPED RODS SUCH AS THESE CAN BE BOUGHT AND ARE THE SIMPLEST TYPE TO USE.

1 TO MAKE A PAIR OF
L-RODS, TAKE TWO WIRE
COATHANGERS. CUT THEM
BELOW THE HOOK AND NEAR
THE OPPOSITE CORNER.

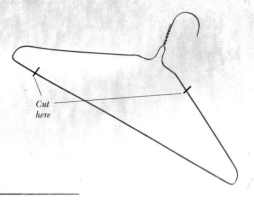

Cut here

Bend to 90°

2 TAKE THE CORNER OF EACH,
WHICH WILL BE AT AN ANGLE OF
ABOUT 45°, AND BEND IT
CAREFULLY THROUGH 90°.

The grip should be steady but not tight

3 WHEN USING THE RODS
HOLD THEM BY THE SHORTER
LENGTH JUST UNDER THE BEND.

4 FOR YOUR OWN
PROTECTION, SAND DOWN
ANY ROUGHNESS AT THE CUT
ENDS OF THE RODS. COVER
THESE WITH A SLEEVE USING
EMPTY PLASTIC PEN TUBES.

Smooth off rough ends

HOW TO USE THE L-RODS

Relax and center yourself using the breath. First, you need to feel how the rods react before aiming for a real target.

Hold the rods in loosely clenched fists with the thumbs resting outside the fingers. Bend your elbows, keep them close to the trunk of the body, and hold the rods parallel and horizontal, about 8in. (20cm) apart from each other and pointing forward.

You are looking for a line that will give a reaction, so walk forward slowly until the rods cross over or open out into a V-shape. Note the point where this happens on the ground. Return to your starting point and repeat the process for confirmation. Once you have established this first point, walk *across* the invisible point until the rods revert to their original position. Turn back at a different angle to the first point to try to track the direction of the line. Each time you get a reaction, mark the place (see diagram, right). Alternatively, stand on your point instead of zig-zagging, turn, and attempt to walk along the line as the rods hold the "found" position.

What have you found? At this point it doesn't matter. Dowsing rods

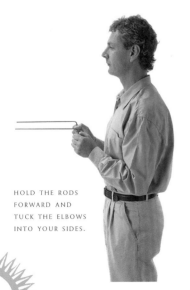

HOLD THE RODS FORWARD AND TUCK THE ELBOWS INTO YOUR SIDES.

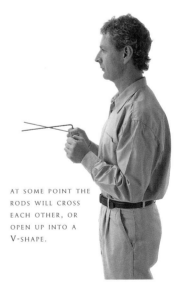

AT SOME POINT THE RODS WILL CROSS EACH OTHER, OR OPEN UP INTO A V-SHAPE.

Walk slowly forward

Note the ground at which point the rods cross

THE GROUND UNDERNEATH WHERE THE
RODS CROSS OVER COULD CONTAIN
WATER, MINERALS, AND EARTH ENERGIES.

will react to almost anything and, in the hands of a beginner, may wave all over the place, which can be disconcerting. So the next step is to seek a real target: find the water pipe entering your house from underneath the road outside. A good place to start is the mains stopcock, which is likely to be under a metal cover on the sidewalk.

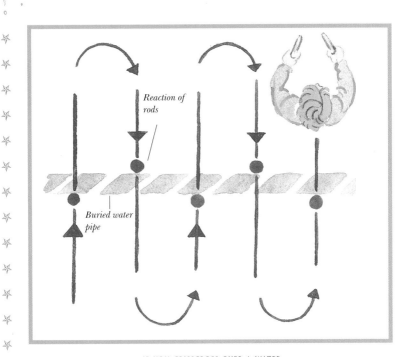

Reaction of rods

Buried water pipe

IF YOU CRISSCROSS OVER A WATER
PIPE THE RODS WILL REACT EACH
TIME YOU PASS OVER IT.

SEEKING A WATER PIPE

 Once you have found the stopcock, position the rods above it. They should react by crossing over each other. If they don't, then this is a chance to program in your own reaction. Say to yourself:

This is water.

and cross the rods yourself. Then say:

I seek the waterpipe into my house.

The rods remain crossed only above the line of the pipe. The point of this exercise is that you should train yourself to remain focused on a known target. Letting your mind wander will signal "wander" to the rods. Mark the line as you progress.

Alternatively, place a broom on the floor and starting at one end, say to yourself "Rods cross over to react to this line." Then track and follow the broom, walking over it. Step aside sometimes so that the rods open. Return to your position above the broom and watch the rods cross back again.

These exercises on known targets help to build confidence when searching for "invisible" targets.

FINDING THE DIRECTION

1. To find which way a pipe or cable is running, stand still over the discovered target and holding one rod in your writing hand say:

Show me the direction.

The single rod should slowly swing and point accordingly.

2. To find the direction of the flow of water or earth-energy line you have located, stand still and say:

Show me from which direction the flow is coming.

Check it with the question:

Show me the direction the flow is going.

Then place indicating markers on the ground.

3. Instead of walking back and forth over a field seeking your target, stand at the edge and using the single rod, ask for the direction in which to proceed. The rod will point the way, so move forward slowly with both rods looking for the crossover reaction. Mark the spot.

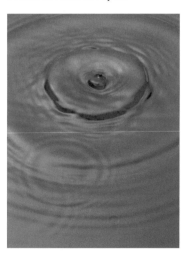

DOWSING WITH RODS IS TRADITIONALLY ASSOCIATED WITH SEARCHING FOR WATER.

THE Y-ROD

This shape is the traditional forked stick associated with water divining and can be made from any material that is supple and springy. Two equal lengths of strong wire or plastic will suffice, well secured together at one end with the other ends held one in each hand.

TO MAKE FROM WOOD

Look for a hazel twig with two branches even in length about 12–15in. (30–40cm) and of equal "chunky pencil" diameter that join a half-inch diameter branch. Cut 6–8in. (15–18cm) below the joint of the twigs to the branch, which then becomes the pointer.

Cut here

ONE HAZEL BRANCH MAY PROVIDE MORE THAN ONE Y-SHAPED ROD WHEN CUT IN THE RIGHT PLACES.

HOW TO USE THE Y-ROD

To hold a Y-rod your palms must face upward with the thumbs lying along the twigs and pointing skyward, the pointer of the rod directed toward the ground. Tuck the elbows into the body and with forearms horizontal, place a little tension between each twig by pulling them gently apart and hold this tension steady so that the pointer is free to move up or down.

The reaction to a target like water can be very strong: the rod twists as it begins to react and then the pointer swings up suddenly and may even hit you on the chest. Practice by walking the ground as described with the L-rods (*see page 24*) and learn your own signals. If you locate a stream of underground water and walk its line, the pointer will usually dip if you are walking with the flow and lift if walking against it. But personal reactions can vary.

EACH TWIG OF THE ROD SHOULD BE HELD WITH A LITTLE TENSION.

THE ROD MAY REACT BY SUDDENLY TURNING UPWARD.

THE ROD WILL START TO MOVE AS YOU COME TO A TARGET, SUCH AS AN UNDERGROUND STREAM.

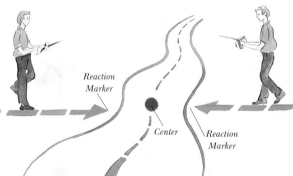

Reaction Marker

Center

Reaction Marker

29

THE BOBBER

 This is a single, springy, tapered rod that can be made of hazelwood or metal and is held at the thin end by one or both hands in front of the body. If it's the longer-length variety, it can be aimed about 12in. (30cm) from the ground. To indicate YES, it usually bobs up and down and for NO it wags from side to side. Obviously you need to check for your own signals or program it before use.

Some types of bobbers have a copper coil or weight on the end. The longer one is like a fishing rod held by the thin end. Short or long ones can be made easily provided you are careful to incorporate the tapered resilience in the rod. It is favored by skilled oil dowsers.

FINDING DEPTH

 The bobber can be used to indicate the depth of a target such as water or a mineral vein. You will use common sense regarding a depth assessment on a chosen target, of course, so start with a realistic idea. For example, hold the bobber over your discovered target point and say:

Is the depth more than 20 feet (6 meters)?

If it bobs YES, then say:

I am counting one bob for every five feet (1.5 meters) – or perhaps 10 feet (3 meters) as you think fit.

Count the number of bobs from the 20 already ascertained thus: "25, 30, 35" etc. until it changes movement from up and down to side to side. Be inventive with your request to save time in counting.

Another way to ascertain depth is the established method called:

BISHOP'S RULE

Distance out equals distance down.

 Stand at the target spot you have found and put down a marker. Ask the instrument to respond for depth. Slowly walk away from the point until you get a positive response. The distance from the marker is equal to the depth.

DOWSING RODS

Some bobbers have a weight at the end

THE BOBBER IS A
TAPERED ROD THAT
BOBS UP AND
DOWN OR WAGS
FROM SIDE TO SIDE.

Found target

Distance out

Distance down is the same as distance out

THE DEPTH OF A
TARGET IS FOUND
BY WALKING AWAY
FROM IT; THE
INSTRUMENT
REACTS AT A
DISTANCE
EQUIVALENT TO
THE DEPTH.

31

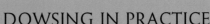

DOWSING IN PRACTICE

There are a number of techniques to help develop your skill as a dowser, from simple games that focus your concentration to experiments with water and the human body.

PENDULUM SOLITAIRE

Shuffle an ordinary deck of playing cards and cut in half. Set aside one half (to reduce the number) and spread out the other, face down on a surface in front of you. Mentally focus on the idea that with the short pendulum you will scan the cards and pick out only picture cards (Jack, Queen, King). Center yourself, check your YES/NO responses, and activate the pendulum into scanning. Then ask:

Is this a picture card?

When the pendulum gives YES, pick up the cards but keep them face down and place in a pile. Once you feel the task is complete, turn them over and check how accurate you were. Make a note of your score.

Then turn up the remainder to see if any picture cards were overlooked.

Keep the score and date in your work journal as a progress check. Move on to using the whole deck when you feel ready.

MEMORY SCANNING

Adapt the party game used by Rudyard Kipling in his mystical novel *Kim* of placing about twenty small articles on a tray and memorizing as many as possible using the pendulum.

Center yourself and check your YES/NO responses. Now pendulum scan over all the articles. Take only three minutes; set a timer.

Cover the tray. Now write a list of the objects in another three minutes. Scan the *covered* tray to trigger your memory if necessary but rerun the scan in your mind when writing down the collection. Increase and change the number of objects for further scanning practice. Develop this exercise by scanning the covered tray to determine each article's substance – wood, brass, glass, and so on.

SHARPEN YOUR SKILLS BY USING A PENDULUM TO IDENTIFY PLAYING CARDS.

SCANNING ARTICLES ON A COVERED TRAY ALSO HELPS TO DEVELOP DOWSING SKILLS.

DECISION-MAKING

 It is difficult sometimes to choose a course of action but by using the short pendulum, you can find that it becomes easier to make decisions. The most common form of indecision is when we are confronted with dual choice and don't know which way to turn.

For example, you are looking through the paper for a new job, or an apartment, a new house, or a used car. Cut out the ads that sound interesting, take the short pendulum, center yourself, and frame the right question. Scan first one by one, and ask:

Is this compatible with me?

Discard those which indicate negative. For the remainder, the next question could be:

Shall I proceed with inquiries?

Adapt this example for any situation or forthcoming event that interests you.

COMPATIBILITY

 Because you are as unique as your fingerprints, you know that what suits one person doesn't always suit another. Dowsing enables you to clarify your thoughts and feelings since the pendulum has become an extension of you, bringing your right and left brain functions into harmony.

RED FIVE-DOOR FAMILY AUTO
Central locking, twin air bags, sunroof, radio cassette, good condition

CAR FOR SALE
Immaculate condition, light gray leather interior, air conditioning, central locking, electronic sunroof. Excellent service history – 27,000 miles.

BLUE CONVERTIBLE
17,000 miles with full service history. Exceptional condition.

THE PENDULUM
CAN GUIDE YOU IN
CHOOSING WHICH
NEW CAR TO BUY.

G RED SPORTSCAR
urious suede interior,
nmobilizer, air con, fantastic
hi-fi, ideal gift. Viewing
Saturday. 37,000 miles—looks
and drives like new.

HEALTH MATTERS

Allergies can be discovered
by scanning your hand as it
rests palm down beside the
suspect food or chemical, then
scanning the sample itself ask:

Is this compatible with me?

You make the link between yourself
and the sample and allow the
pendulum to respond YES or NO.
The sample can also be held in the
free hand and questioned. The same
simple exercise can be used to test
your sensitivity to certain house-
hold cleaning products, makeup,
perfumes – in fact, just about
anything. Record your findings.

DOWSING CAN HELP
IDENTIFY ALLERGIES
TO COMMONLY
USED PRODUCTS.

FIND OUT WHETHER TAP WATER, FILTERED WATER, OR BOTTLED WATER SUITS YOU.

WATER

Does it suit you? In order to test fresh or filtered water, scan a small sample of each beside your free hand, palm down in the same way as in the compatibility test. Sometimes a YES/But, NO/But response occurs with this inquiry, so in readiness have your next question prepared:

Am I allergic to something in this water?

Do conduct a sensible experiment and make detailed notes, but remember that the effect may be different for other people due to individual levels of tolerance.

THE HUMAN BODY

Dowsing techniques are used as a diagnostic tool worldwide by qualified practitioners of healing and complementary medicine who treat the body holistically by examining the anatomy, physiology, chakras, meridians, and subtle body systems of the patient.

Radionic therapeutics is a type of diagnosis and treatment that can be given from a distance through radiesthesia, by letter or telephone, for example. The name radiesthesia describes dowsing with rods or pendulum to determine individual treatment through a blood or hair sample from the patient which is called a 'witness'.

MANY COMPLEMENTARY THERAPISTS INCLUDE DOWSING TECHNIQUES IN THEIR HOLISTIC APPROACH TO DIAGNOSIS.

If you have worked well at your response-ability, try pendulum dowsing over some homeopathic remedies, flower essences, and aromatherapy oils in order to select what is currently suitable for you. Remember, the remedy that worked last time may be ineffective now. Place the test item on your free palm and ask questions such as:

Is this remedy suitable for me?
Do I need this remedy?

Alternatively, place the bottle or container in question beside your hand and scan as you would for allergy testing. Use this exercise to research any product you are thinking of using. You can also write down a list of vitamins and scan them, or scan advertisements in newspapers or magazines to check what is right for you.

• Vitamin A
• Vitamin C
• Vitamin B12
• Vitamin E
• Vitamin B6
• Vitamin D

DOWSING MAY DETERMINE WHETHER A PARTICULAR REMEDY, VITAMIN, OR PRODUCT IS RIGHT FOR YOU.

ASTROLOGY

 The precise time of birth is crucial when preparing a birth chart but it is surprising how seldom this gets recorded. Many professional astrologers practice dowsing to gain this information. There are a number of simple ways to do this, such as writing down the name of the person and scanning it, then asking:

Can I have the time of birth of this person?

YES. (If NO, then you should leave it and try again later.)

Here is a typical set of questions and answers:

Is it morning? NO. Is it afternoon? NO. Is it evening? YES. After 6p.m.? YES. After 7p.m.? NO. Between 6 and 6:30p.m.? YES. Between 6 and 6:15p.m.? YES. Between 6 and 6:05p.m.? NO. 6:05 and 6:10p.m.? YES. Then slowly ask: 6:06? 6:07? and wait for the pendulum to respond.

In this way, an exact time can be achieved, which is doubly important where twins are concerned!

THE UNBORN CHILD

 If you wish to learn the sex of a baby before birth, and before the hospital scan, place the hand of the mother-to-be face-down and scan it with the short pendulum. Then ask:

Can I ask the sex of this unborn child? YES. Is the child male?

Don't be alarmed if you get YES/But ... There may be more than one baby! Of course, you ask if there is more than one. This test conducted too early in the pregnancy can also give a NO response.

DOWSING CAN HELP YOU PREDICT THE PRECISE TIME OF BIRTH — EVEN FOR TWINS.

YOU ARE MORE
LIKELY TO GET
A SUCCESSFUL
PREDICTION OF THE
SEX OF THE UNBORN
CHILD LATER IN THE
PREGNANCY.

EXTENDING YOUR SKILLS

When you have mastered the basic skills of dowsing you can progress to using the color disk and the long pendulum.

THE MAGER ROSETTE

 Using circles or disks as indicators is a helpful focus for getting certain information.

In the early 1900s, a Frenchman, Professor Henri Mager, invented a disk called the Mager Rosette which uses colors to indicate contamination in water. To make one, cut out a circle from cardboard – about 3in. (6–7cm) in diameter – and divide the circle into eight equal sections. Color each section: (*see page 41*).

1 Violet, PURE
2 Blue, NORMAL for drinking
3 Green, MINERALS present
4 Yellow, HARD WATER SALTS
5 Red, IRON
6 Gray, LOW QUALITY/POLLUTED (possibly lead)
7 Black, AVOID!
8 White, HEALING

Hold the pendulum in your working hand and hold the color disk with the selected color between the thumb and forefinger; dowse over a water sample or above a previously located water source.

If a quick "quality control" for water is required, perhaps in a restaurant, use the pendulum to give points out of ten. Merely ask the pendulum to respond YES to the correct number as you give the countdown! You can also match the colors on the disk to points on the compass. When working outdoors, take a compass reading to find north. The color violet responds to north, red to south, green to east, and black to west. This could prove useful if you lose your direction and you have no compass.

Again, using the Mager color-coding disk, test for reaction over a collection of substances one by one such as brass (ornament), copper (coin), iron (nail), plastic, glass, etc., and establish your own color code for minerals and substances.

When testing, bear in mind that yellow reacts to sulfur, and red reacts to iron; this can be useful for diagnosing water content.

THE MAGER ROSETTE, INVENTED IN THE EARLY 1900s, IS ESPECIALLY USEFUL FOR TESTING WATER.

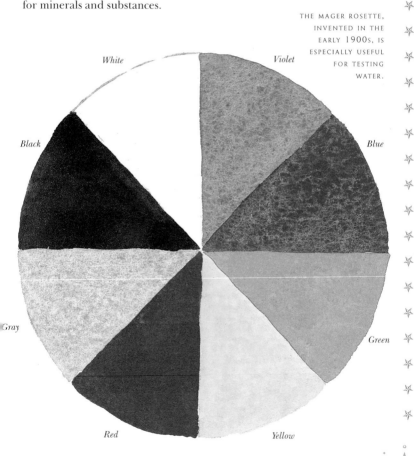

White

Violet

Blue

Black

Gray

Green

Red

Yellow

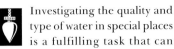

SACRED WELLS AND SPRINGS

 Investigating the quality and type of water in special places is a fulfilling task that can sometimes bring unexpected information. Water has its own code or signature, which you can discover simply by asking for it, using the short pendulum over the sample. Let the pendulum scan the liquid as you pose the question and then count the number and direction of gyrations or oscillations in the sequence. This pattern is the signature of that particular sacred water. It may have a tradition or reputation for healing properties so try comparing signatures with water samples from other sites.

You can also find the signatures of crystals such as clear quartz, amethyst quartz, and rose quartz.

Try leaving a quartz crystal in tested pure water for 24 hours, then test the water again for any changes.

THE LONG PENDULUM

T.C. Lethbridge was an archeologist who also pioneered specialist dowsing techniques. He found substances and concepts both have different rates of resonance, revealed by varying the length of cord attached to a wooden pendulum. For example, slate and concrete respond to a cord length of 13in. (33cm). Silver, lead, calcium, and sodium to 22in.(56cm). Gold to 29in.(74cm). Copper and cobalt to 30.5in. (77cm). Iron to 32in. (81cm) and nickel to 32.5in. (82cm). Try this by scanning the object and unwinding the string until the pendulum moves in a circle. This is the corresponding length for the substance. Mark the string at the appropriate point.

Lethbridge's measurement for the abstract quality of light was 10in. (25cm). He also found measurements for: life force – 20in. (50cm); male principle – 24in. (61cm); female – 29in. (74cm); sound – 30 in. (76cm), and sleep/death – 40in (102cm). Experiment with this and improve your researching techniques.

THE SPECIAL FEATURES
OF CRYSTALS CAN BE
ASCERTAINED BY TESTING
PURE WATER IN WHICH
THEY HAVE BEEN LEFT
FOR A DAY.

1 HOLD THE PENDULUM BY A SHORT LENGTH OVER YOUR CHOSEN MATERIAL.

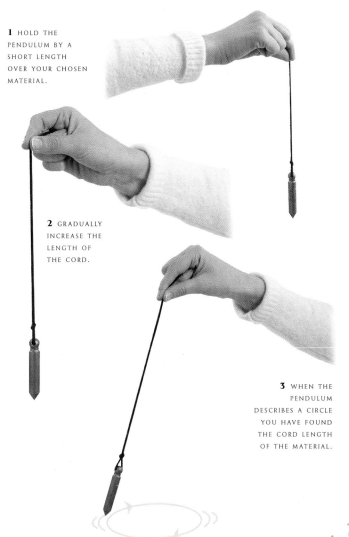

2 GRADUALLY INCREASE THE LENGTH OF THE CORD.

3 WHEN THE PENDULUM DESCRIBES A CIRCLE YOU HAVE FOUND THE CORD LENGTH OF THE MATERIAL.

ADVANCED SKILLS

Using a pendulum to dowse maps, plans, and photos at home is a special technique that yields exciting results. You can scan ancient battlesites, conduct housing surveys, and even search for missing persons.

MAP DOWSING

Preliminary ground surveys can be conducted for any point on the globe without leaving your chair. These are carried out for mineral and water searches as a rule but dowsing experts are used regularly for archeological, geological, and geopathic purposes as well as looking for missing persons. Your own search could reflect personal interests and include historical locations such as ancient battlesites, buildings, and wells or springs and river sources – the choice is yours.

Map dowsing extends mental concentration and focuses the mind on an area through the coordinates of its location on a map in front of you. Hold the pendulum in the strong hand and a pointer (perhaps a pencil) in the other. Be clear in your mind before you go about dowsing your chosen target.

First scan with the pendulum down the side of the map until you get a positive response. Mark it. Then scan across the top of the map for the positive response and mark that too. Draw a line with a ruler from each point, and your target area is where the lines cross.

Another task is to select and section off an area on the map within which to work. Scan it systematically using the pointer to mark your track and hold the target firmly in mind. The pendulum can be held comfortably away from the area – the pointer directs while the pendulum responds. Use a tape recorder to record your questions and findings.

AN AREA ON THE
OTHER SIDE OF THE
GLOBE CAN BE
DOWSED WITH ONLY A
MAP, PENDULUM, AND
POINTER.

*Pass the
pendulum
down the side
of the map*

*Mark the
points where
the pendulum
reacts*

IMAGES

The same type of map-dowsing technique can be used for exploring maps of a different kind: photographs, drawings, and architectural plans. Photographs of missing people can be dowsed to try to find them but this does need excellent questioning skill and a sound ethical approach. Toward the end of the Vietnam war a naval captain organized a dowsing group who successfully located survivors of a ship sunk in a battle as well as finding other lost and wandering Vietnamese refugees.

If you are seeking a new home it's a good idea to dowse a photograph of the prospective property. Careful thought beforehand to plan your questions is once again the key to successful research.

> *Is the structure sound?*
> *Is it a fair price?*
> *What year was it built?*
> *Has anyone died there?*
> *Are there any geopathic stress lines*
> *entering the house?*

Examples like these may well suggest additional questions about size, age, and value.

WHEN THINKING OF BUYING A NEW HOME ACQUIRE A PHOTOGRAPH OF IT AND DOWSE IT.

JONES
REAL
ESTATE

A FIVE BEDROOMED HOUSE

This handsome home in the lovely Riverside area has easy access to public transportation, restaurants, and shops.

HALLWAY: Spacious hallway with polished hardwood floor and elegant wood moldings.

LIVING ROOM: Light and airy room with views to backyard. Walls and paintwork in good condition, stunning mantel fireplace and pinewood ceiling.

ARCHITECTURAL PLANS, DESIGNS, AND DRAWINGS

Plans of buildings both old and new are often dowsed for water pipes, electricity systems, or even hidden wells. Drawing a plan of your own home to determine what lies beneath, around, and within it can reveal helpful and fascinating facts using the map-dowsing methods.

If you have studied Feng Shui, the ancient Chinese art of geomancy that manipulates invisible energy lines, you will know that there is a plan known as a ba-gua that is placed over a dwelling; the ba-gua is an octagonal arrangement of trigrams used in I Ching divination. Dowsing on the ba-gua sections to find areas of the house that need attention will pinpoint them instantly by using the pendulum.

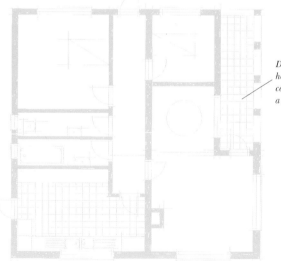

Dowsing house plans could reveal a hidden well

PLANS OF BOTH OLD AND NEW BUILDINGS CAN BE DOWSED FOR HIDDEN HAZARDS.

THE INVISIBLE LANDSCAPE

Invisible to the naked eye, the landscape is patterned with hidden energy lines know as "leys." Ancient peoples sited their roads, temples, and tombs around these leys, and you can map them for yourself by dowsing.

SEARCHING FOR LEY LINES

So far, we have explored dowsing for physical subjects, such as pipes and water, which are known, or thought, to exist in a certain area. Then we moved into sensing and intuiting with the pendulum through images and map-dowsing techniques. Now, looking at the landscape, we use these skills plus an open mind to bring the invisible into focus.

Alignments between ancient sites in the English countryside were discovered by Alfred Watkins in 1921, and his findings were later published in *The Old Straight Track* in 1925. He called these tracks ley lines, derived from the Saxon "ley," but believed these connecting lines were used efficiently by Neolithic

THE ENGLISH COUNTRYSIDE IS CRISS-CROSSED WITH HIDDEN LEY LINES.

people (4000–2000 B.C.E.), who built the long barrow burial mounds through to the Bronze and Iron Ages. The original "knowledge" faded but the energy points were still active during the Roman occupation of Britain and in ancient tracks taken over for road building.

Mounds, barrows, tombs, cairns, dolmens, wells, standing stones, stone circles, ancient crosses, churches, and chapels were all seen by Watkins in a new light once he had noticed these alignments.

He researched many of the ancient places along the alignments and found other connections such as marker stones and more dowsable lines that joined the originals. So what had he "unearthed?"

The building of Christian churches on earlier pagan sacred sites was obviously a factor in this but it is clear that the earth's invisible energies that bring harmony and power to the landscape were also being utilized.

The avid dowsing researcher will find that these buildings themselves supply an amazing amount of information in addition to that printed in the official guides.

ANCIENT SITES ARE OFTEN JOINED BY ENERGY LINES DETECTABLE IN DOWSING.

ENERGY LINES
AND SACRED CENTERS

 Since Alfred Watkins' day, investigations of archeological and earth-energy sites have developed and spread across the surface of the globe as researchers use a variety of dowsing methods to make observations and conduct experiments that have contributed valuable information about ancient civilizations and historical sites.

Dowsing has revealed that primary underground water is always present at important sites such as stone circles. This water is created by mineral reactions deep in the earth, forced upward and sideways through rock fissures into what are called "blind springs" or "domes." Sometimes, a break-through has occurred where ancient wells, springs, or waterfalls have been found. The ancient peoples who built sacred centers over primary water and aligned them with seasonally occurring astronomical features had a knowledge that respected the laws of nature and understood how to use land-energy for a productive and harmonious life. Their scientific approach is inconceivable to modern people.

More recently, dowsers have discovered other features such as positive or negative energy flows that run along, or close to, major alignment ley lines. The Michael and Mary lines in England are a good example of "male–female" energy flows that follow close to the May 1st sunrise alignment that weaves from the southwest of the country to the east and has been diligently plotted by Hamish Miller and Paul Broadhurst for their book, *The Sun and the Serpent*.

THE SOUTH OF ENGLAND REVEALS LEY LINES THAT FOLLOW THE PATH OF THE SUNRISE ON MAY 1ST.

POINTS TO REMEMBER

An earth-energy dowser needs to have acquired some idea of the following:

1. The complexities of underground water systems.
2. The differences between straight-alignment ley lines and other detectable ground energies. Are they natural or artificial?
3. The directions taken by positive and negative energy flows.
4. The "power" emanating from natural stone.

Consider joining a group or finding a teacher to help you with the basic technique before opening yourself up to energies that can sometimes be physically depleting.

KEY TO MAP

1. Carn Les Boel
2. St. Michael's Mount
3. Cheesewring
4. St. Michael's Church
5. St. Michael's Church, Trull
6. Burrowbridge Mump
7. St. Michael's Church, Othery
8. Glastonbury
9. Stoke St. Michael Church
10. Avebury
11. Ogbourne St. George
12. St. Michael's Church, Clifton Hampden
13. Royston
14. Bury St. Edmunds
15. St. Margaret's Church, Hopton

DOWSING AND GEOPATHIC STRESS

Subterranean energy fields affect the health and well-being of us all. Check out your home for negative energy lines or interference zones that may be damaging your health.

HOW NEGATIVE ENERGY DAMAGES YOUR HEALTH

 Where two subterranean water courses are found to cross at different levels, that spot is called an interference zone. Such zones, as well as geological faults, negative underground streams, and radiation, we now know are detrimental to human health and well-being. Fretful babies, many people suffering from insomnia, and children who are constantly unwell have been found to have their beds positioned over interference zones or subterranean streams. When the sufferer's cot or bed was moved, their problems went away.

These zones or negative energy lines can affect upper floors of buildings as well as the ground levels.

Dowsers are often called in as a last resort when a house or building has a persistently damp area: perhaps wood rot has been found although the building is structurally sound with no leaking roof and faultless damp-proofing. The cause, geopathic stress, can usually be located by the professional dowser where other technologies have failed. The dowser will divert or change the negative energy flow that is entering the building.

New buildings erected on ancient sites can be affected by the memory vibrations left behind by former occupants of the land or the previous buildings. Ghost hunters please note! When this happens, a search of land usage should be made and a clearance may be carried out by a specialist.

ENERGIES CAUSE HEALING AND HARM

Some historical buildings or ruins carry artificial lines created by using existing natural ground forces and reconstructing them into positive centers that revitalized the occupants, perhaps for healing, or gave beneficial power to buildings that were used for religious purposes, such as churches or chapels. But the reverse sometimes happens. Many years ago in Germany, an accident black-spot was examined by several experienced dowsers who found that it was a severe interference zone that had been worsened by the very construction of the autobahn itself.

A NEGATIVE ENERGY LINE MAY BE AFFECTING YOUR CHILD'S HEALTH.

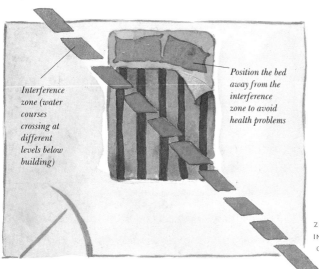

Interference zone (water courses crossing at different levels below building)

Position the bed away from the interference zone to avoid health problems

PLACING A BED NEAR AN INTERFERENCE ZONE MAY RESULT IN INSOMNIA AND OTHER AILMENTS.

CONCLUSION

 By perseverance and constant practice of the basic dowsing procedures you will extend your skills through imaginative, simple, and specific questions, and develop a useful *response-ability* to improve the quality of your life and that of others.

Give yourself time to experiment and always record your findings. Above all, be patient.

Working with or learning from an experienced or professional dowser can make all the difference. Get in touch with a national or local society for information. In my own case, I have been inspired by the skills of Hamish Miller, have worked briefly with the great British dowser from Devon, John Bower, and gratefully received sensitive dowsing support from Julian MacKerricher of Nottinghamshire.

Dowsing skills can support and improve your knowledge of other interests and hobbies while considerably developing your awareness of and sensitivity to the world around you.

The days are past when dowsing belonged only to the rustic water diviner, plodding the fields with a forked stick. More and more people, organizations, and businesses have realized the potential for making useful discoveries that dowsing offers. Although we do not have a scientific explanation for how dowsing works, the results speak for themselves and confirm that it is a successful and extremely rewarding occupation on every level.

Children respond naturally to dowsing techniques and should be encouraged to try dowsing games and treasure hunts. It makes a change from computer games and brings a family together to work on projects, such as searches for water, minerals, and old wells, or dowsing ancient battlefields or settlements. The list of uses to which you can put dowsing is endless. All you need is a little imagination to start you on your quest. Good luck.

FURTHER READING

DEVEREUX, Paul, *The New Ley Hunter's Guide* (Gothic Image, 1994)

GRAVES, Tom, *Discover Dowsing* (Aquarian Press, 1993)

LETHBRIDGE, T.C., *Ghost & Divining Rod* (Routledge & Kegan Paul, 1963)

LONEGREN, Sig, *Spiritual Dowsing* (Gothic Image, 1986)

MILLER, Hamish, BROADHURST, Paul, *The Sun and the Serpent* (Pendragon Press, 1989)

WHITLOCK, Ralph, *Water Divining* (Robert Hale, 1992)

USEFUL ADDRESSES

THE BRITISH SOCIETY OF DOWSERS,
Sycamore Barn, Hastingleigh,
Ashford, Kent,
England
TN25 5HW
Tel/Fax: 01233 750253
e-mail: bsd@dowsers.demon.co.uk
Web site: www.dowsers.demon.co.uk

With thanks to the British Society of Dowsing for the loan of equipment and photographs.

Founded in 1933, the B.S.D. is a major national organization and registered charity. It publishes a quarterly journal and keeps a register of practicing dowsers. It has a lending/reference library.

RADIONICS ASSOCIATION,
Baerlin House,
Goose Green,
Deddington,
Oxford
OX5 4SZ
Tel/Fax: 01869 338852

THE FAMED BRITISH
DOWSER HAMISH
MILLER AT WORK IN
CORNWALL BY
ST. MICHAEL'S MOUNT.

INDEX

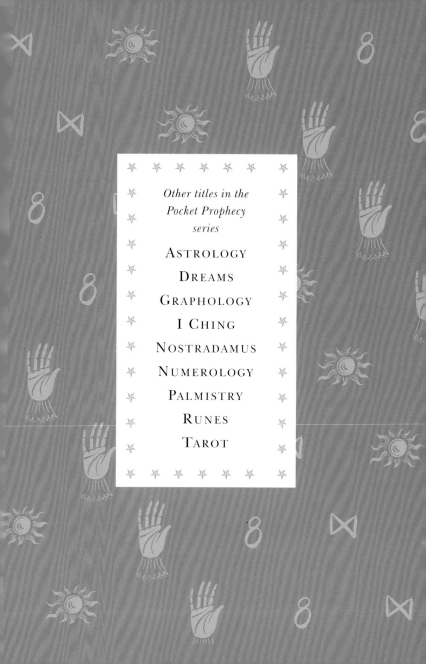